𝍫 ||

counting the cost

Essential Truths to Answering God's Call

DR. JOELLE SUEL

𝍦 ||
counting the cost
Essential Truths to Answering God's Call

TATE PUBLISHING *& Enterprises*

Counting the Cost
Copyright © 2010 by Dr. Joelle Suel. All rights reserved.

No part of this publication may be reproduced, stored in a retrieval system or transmitted in any way by any means, electronic, mechanical, photocopy, recording or otherwise without the prior permission of the author except as provided by USA copyright law.

Scripture quotations are taken from the *Holy Bible, King James Version,* Cambridge, 1769. Used by permission. All rights reserved.

The opinions expressed by the author are not necessarily those of Tate Publishing, LLC.

Published by Tate Publishing & Enterprises, LLC
127 E. Trade Center Terrace | Mustang, Oklahoma 73064 USA
1.888.361.9473 | www.tatepublishing.com

Tate Publishing is committed to excellence in the publishing industry. The company reflects the philosophy established by the founders, based on Psalm 68:11,
"The Lord gave the word and great was the company of those who published it."

Book design copyright © 2010 by Tate Publishing, LLC. All rights reserved.
Cover design by Kellie Southerland
Interior design by Stephanie Woloszyn

Published in the United States of America

ISBN: 978-1-61566-777-2
1. Religion / Christian Life / Personal Growth
2. Religion / Christian Life / Spiritual Growth
10.02.09

To all those whose hearts are set on knowing,
understanding, pursuing, and obeying the call of God.
May you have the assurance that your labor of love
is not in vain in the Lord. Knowing others are also
pressing through the pressure has helped me to stand.
Indeed we can testify, "Faithful *is* he that calleth you,
who also will do *it*" (1 Thessalonians 5:24).
May all hindrances be removed as you
continue to obey him from glory to glory!

acknowledgments

First and foremost, I give praise, honor, and glory to God, apart from whom I can do nothing. I love you, Lord.

Special thanks to those who contributed to the work of this book. Your dedication and spirit of excellence have been remarkable.

My heartfelt appreciation and love go out to all who have influenced, encouraged, and supported me in my pursuit of kingdom purpose. *Merci!*

table of contents

Introduction	11
Death	15
Discipleship	21
Dedication	29
Destination	41
Divers Temptations	51
Determination	61
Divine Endowment	67
Conclusion	75
Nuggets of Truth	79

introduction

There are kingdom steps that helped me and continue to guide me in accomplishing what the Lord leads me to do. These are understood deeper and deeper at each level of growth from glory to glory, faith to faith, and strength to strength. My heart's desire is to share these in order to encourage, build up, and edify the body of Christ.

Truly, the Holy Spirit led every phase of writing this book. From conception to completion, he guided even the unseen details. I remember how he gave me the seven chapter titles one by one in a very specific order. That order is of great importance and is a message in itself. Each step leads to the next and works together with the others. The first chapter, "Death," in the natural, should be the last. The last chapter, "Divine Endowment," is often sought after first. However, it comes at the end because its increase results from what precedes it.

The order of these steps is as important as the order in which we answer the call of God on our lives. Where do we start? Do we continue what we were doing? Do we stop and start all over again? What does it take to serve the Most High God? In Luke 12:48 we read, "For unto whomsoever much is given, of him shall be much required." The requirements outlined in the chapters you are about to read, if followed, will assure the fruit of what has been given to you. They will water the seeds that have been planted in your vineyard.

After the titles came the key scriptures for each chapter, all pertaining to *counting*. They contain the same word: *count. Count* comes from the Greek word *logizomai,* meaning to reckon, consider, suppose, or to think on. Each chapter covers a principle connected to this meaning. Meditating on these essential truths enables us to make decisions with great determination.

The Lord tells us in Luke 14:28, "For which of you, intending to build a tower, sitteth not down first, and *counteth the cost,* whether he have sufficient to finish it?" Herein lays the content of this book: *Counting the Cost.* The Lord will use these words to bring forth the purpose he has for you for such a time as this. Each time you read it, more will be revealed to you.

COUNTING THE COST

Prepare yourself for the challenge of walking in God's strength, being encouraged by his love, and putting on his authority like a garment. The revelation of your identity in Christ lies within your willingness to die to everything that pertains to you apart from him. The glory of death is the power of the resurrection being manifest fully in you through the Holy Spirit. What greater honor is there than to be a vessel of honor for the Lord of glory?

> Likewise reckon ye also yourselves to be dead indeed unto sin, but alive unto God through Jesus Christ our Lord.
>
> Romans 6:11

As the war between the flesh and the Spirit rages on, we are plunged into despair when we try to conquer a stronghold, and it binds us even more. We experience turmoil when we are unable to stop doing what we no longer desire to do! What is the answer to this battle?

To *reckon* means to ac*count* for, to *count* something as done, to conclude an act completed. Chapter 6 of Romans emphasizes this truth. It is necessary to implement it in order to win the war with our flesh and walk in the Spirit, as further explained in chapters 7 and 8. We cannot *count* ourselves to be alive unto God through Jesus Christ our Lord without first *counting* ourselves

death

as being dead unto sin. Spiritually, we have been crucified with the Lord. Therefore, in the same manner, we identify with his resurrection. There cannot be a resurrection if there is no crucifixion. Death to the flesh is a very important milestone in our walk. The timing of it differs for every one of us. When death occurs, we never forget it. Death takes us into another realm of experiencing the reality of the life of Christ in us. The Spirit of Christ leads us to that place of death to the flesh as he reveals truths accomplished through the cross. These truths become alive to us when we recognize ourselves nailed there as well. The cross becomes the crossroad between the flesh and the Spirit.

We know we have died to ourselves when it is no longer our will but his will we want accomplished. At the place where we come to the end of ourselves, he *then* begins. When we are willing to do whatever it takes to obey him, regardless of the cost, he *then* steps in. As we give up, he *then* takes us up to another level of trust. After we have tried things our own way and are ready to allow him to have his way, he *then* leads the way. How glorious to die daily so that he can live!

Personally, from that dying moment on, I was able to be led by the Spirit with surety in my steps; that was a turning point in my life. Death to self changed my outlook on everything around me; selfishness and self-centeredness started fading away, and Christ-centeredness increased. It was no longer about me, but about him. From glory to glory, I yielded to his blessed touch and learned to flow with his waves of glory. Moment by moment I learned and continue to learn how to let him be and to decrease that he may increase. Oh, to be launched into the depths of complete surrender!

> I am crucified with Christ: nevertheless I live; yet not I, but Christ liveth in me: and the life which I now live in the flesh I live by the faith of the Son of God, who loved me, and gave himself for me.
>
> Galatians 2:20

The illustration of jumping from an airplane and trusting the parachute to open when necessary is the best way I can describe the step of faith God requires of all his servants. It is easier to stay in the plane, even if we fear it will crash. Although God has many parachutes prepared for us, he will open them only when needed. The ripcord to release them is in his hands. We are not to question or fear that he might not supply our parachute in time. His life is activated outside the airplane of our own life. The plane represents our comfort zone, past failures as well as successes, familiarity, circumstances, and anything else that represents our own life lived for us alone. Oh yes, we can relate to Paul in the previous scripture and truly say, "He gave himself for me. Now surely, I can give my life to him and trust him with it because it is his!"

Death to our flesh, just like natural death, should not be feared. Our Lord took the sting out of death, and through the cross, we have eternal life. We *reckon* to have been crucified with Christ already but have to die daily to appropriate this great truth.

To die daily is like jumping out of the airplane. At times we find ourselves back in the plane. We return there quickly without recognizing it when our loved ones are still on board and are in trouble. It seems the only way to help them is to go where they are, but actually, when we remain outside their plane, they will jump out themselves.

Our getting back into the plane also takes place because we look at the ground and the fear of falling grips us. When we set our mind on earthly things instead of seeking those things that are above, doubt that the parachute will deploy occurs. In addition, when someone calls us from the plane and invites us to return, what appears to be the answer to the loneliness we might be feeling causes our immediate response. When we find ourselves on the plane again, let us quickly get back into the spirit realm. Oh, to be in the realm of his glory!

Seeing the parachutes God makes available to us will help others reach out to him. Parachutes are all the things he brings to prevent our fall. They are the ways of escape he makes when we see the ground and the supernatural release of provision when our vision is blurred by worry. His parachute is the helping hand, the second wind, the last-minute answer, and the manifestation of his glory, suddenly from faith to faith.

For to me to live is Christ, and to die is gain.

Philippians 1:21

Christ is to be our life, the one who reproduces his life in us. When he becomes our motive for ministry, doors open for him, not us. All has to be done for his glory and his alone. The Apostle Paul was determined to see the glory of Christ manifested through him for the furtherance of the gospel and the honor of his name. We should also desire the same. However, it is not something that we do ourselves. It must come forth from within.

One last thing to mention is this: the burial must be complete. In the natural, we do not bury one arm of a dead person, then the other arm, then a foot the next day, then the other a month later. We put the whole body under the ground. So it is to be done with death to the flesh. We cannot bury only a part of us at a time.

Water baptism is a perfect application of this principle. We have to dip our whole body into the water. In doing so, we identify with the death of our Lord on the cross and consider the things of the old man we are now dead to. Rising out of the water in newness of life, we identify with his resurrection. Understanding this principle, I experienced freedom from my addiction to smoking. As I prepared a bath at home that day and went in the water, I pictured the person I used to be before being born again, the old man, dead, which included the cigarettes. Then I got out of the water seeing the new man rise. After years of trying everything to quit smoking, I was finally totally free. There were no withdrawal symptoms. This experience was one of the results of reckoning the old man to be dead and totally buried. We have to put off all of the body in order to put on all of Christ. It is easier to tell a part that comes back up from the grave that it is dead and to go back where it came from than to go through the process of putting to death again what is dead already. What freedom there is when at last we walk in newness of life, his resurrection power!

For which of you, intending to build a tower, sitteth not down first, and counteth the cost, whether he have sufficient to finish it? Lest haply, after he hath laid the foundation, and is not able to finish it, all that behold it begin to mock him, saying, This man began to build, and was not able to finish. Or what king, going to make war against another king, sitteth not down first, and consulteth whether he be able with ten thousand to meet him that cometh against him with twenty thousand? Or else, while the other is yet a great way off, he sendeth ambassadors, and desireth conditions of peace. So likewise, whosoever he be of you that forsaketh not all that he hath, he cannot be my disciple.

Luke 14:28–33

In order to accurately *count the cost*, it is necessary to know what we possess now. What is needed to reach a

II

discipleship

future position cannot be calculated without knowing where we are currently. A step could be missed in the process and hinder what we are to possess. Truth in our assessment of what is *now* will help us speed the process of where we are going.

For every purchase a price has been determined. Before the item is bought, consideration is made of its value. As Christians, we have been bought with a precious price: the blood of our Lord Jesus Christ that was shed on the cross; we belong to him. God valued us that much, and the blood was freely given to us. Our salvation was purchased through the cross, and we have free access to it. The cost of discipleship is another matter. Christ died for us so we could live. Now we have to die for him so he can live through us. In order to obtain our inheritance, we must forsake all. Since we already belong to Jesus, all we can do is surrender.

It is when we can no longer *count* on ourselves that we can *count* on his grace, faithfulness, strength, ability, and power. He will make a way when there is none. We start from point zero and die to possess all of him and none of us. Remember in Galatians 2:20, " I am crucified with Christ, nevertheless I live, yet not I, but Christ who lives in me."

It *costs* us everything to follow him, to pick up our cross is to deny ourselves and acknowledge him. When we start with nothing, we do not have to fear losing something. When we, and all we have, belong to the Lord, we do not have to worry about how to keep it.

Starting a race is one thing; it is another to finish it. We need to sit down and *count the cost* as we walk by faith, moment by moment. This does not imply procrastination in answering the call but indicates that opposition can be expected and perils en*count*ered. When things come upon us suddenly, fear comes. To expect the unexpected helps us grow in awareness. When our house is built upon a rock, the floods come, the winds blow and beat upon it, but it cannot fall because the foundation is sure. We can *count* on having to bear our cross to accomplish whatever he asks us to do. It is easier to build when our only sure foundation is him, having given our all to him to begin with. We can then forsake all for his sake. It is also important not to give up when victory doesn't come as quickly as we think it should. Never stop starting. We are to keep on keeping on.

Let us further comprehend what this discipleship entails. It is only to the extent in which we are a disciple that we can teach others to be so. What we do portrays a greater message than what we say. To make disciples is the main mandate of the Great Commission given to us by our Lord Jesus Christ. The Greek word for disciple is *mathetes*, which comes from the word *matheo*, meaning to learn, or *mathano*, meaning a learner, or pupil. Our Lord is our Master. He leads; we follow. We do not go our own way and ask him to follow us. Willingness to be taught the newness of life in which we are to walk requires us to deny ourselves, our familiar steps, and our former conduct. In other words, we have to say no to the former in order to say yes to the new. We must become and remain teachable. Humility is the gateway to knowing him.

> But ye have not so learned Christ; If so be that ye have heard him, and have been taught by him, as the truth is in Jesus: That ye put off concerning the former conversation the old man, which is corrupt according to the deceitful lusts; And be renewed in the spirit of your mind; And that ye put on the new man, which after God is created in righteousness and true holiness.
>
> Ephesians 4:20–24

It is when we put on that we put off. The Lord teaches us his Word as we walk in the truth of it. The truth that we know sets us free to the point that we walk in it so that the Word may manifest himself through us. We hear the Word, but in doing it, the truth it carries brings renewal to the spirit of our mind. The new man, created in righteousness and true holiness, cannot live apart from the vine to which it belongs. As we abide in him and his words abide in us, we bear much fruit. He is glorified, and we are his disciples indeed. Prior to telling us to *count the cost*, the Lord said,

> If any man come to me, and hate not his father, and mother, and wife, and children, and brethren, and sisters, yea, and his own life also, he cannot be my disciple. And whosoever doth not bear his cross, and come after me, cannot be my disciple.
>
> Luke 14:26–27

We need to understand the effect our discipleship will have on others in order for them not to interfere. This is not only death to self as seen previously, but death to others that will be required. Death to others does not mean that we are dead to others but that others are dead to us in the sense that they are no longer a source of life for us. Before we are born again, what we think is life is not. Our being alive is determined by others, and the result is often disappointment. We live up or down based on our expectations; those being from self or others can only bring us to an appearance of fulfillment. Others are no longer responsible for our happiness. When we start walking in the newness of life, we realize that what *was* can no longer *be.* As we recognize that Christ has become our life, we grow from the place of him being *a part* of our life to him *being* life. Then his life becomes what connects us to others and flows between all relationships, bringing true fulfillment. What is dead *to* us, then, is what is dead in us and others. Every relationship we have must be of a lesser priority than our relationship with him. It does not mean that we do not care about others. On the contrary, his love can flow more freely in and through us to others when they can no longer hinder our oneness with him.

We cannot seek God's approval and man's at the same time. Our goal has to be that we are pleasing to God and not to mankind. To be free from people's acceptance and approval causes a breakthrough of holy boldness in our lives. I call it the "Teflon Anointing." Teflon describes the pots and pans that are nonstick. Offenses as well as compliments have to drop off. If they "stick," they, instead of the Holy Spirit, will start leading us. We have to shake off hindrances and stick with it until they no longer stick.

In conclusion, regarding this important step in answering his call, we observe over and over again that as disciples, as we abide in him, we will ask what we will and it shall be done unto us (John 15:7–8). What a promise!

To remain teachable has been one of my personal daily prayers. In doing so, the more I learn, the more I realize I do not know anything. Any word he reveals to me, he continues to reveal anew at different heights of his glory. When I think I have reached 100-percent depth on a word, he gently shows me it is only 40 percent! The word that abides in me continues to grow as I let him add to it. Selah!

> But what things were gain to me, those I counted loss for Christ. Yea doubtless, and I count all things but loss for the excellency of the knowledge of Christ Jesus my Lord: for whom I have suffered the loss of all things, and do count them but dung, that I may win Christ.
>
> Philippians 3:7–8

Paul clearly *counts* as rubbish the knowledge, experience, understanding, and wisdom he acquired prior to his born-again experience. In doing so, his knowledge of Christ increased and was released. God uses the things of our past for his glory. He has a way of bringing to nothing all things of our past so that he can be our everything. Then God uses those things to testify to others. He uses for his glory what we have gained when we no longer depend on what we know. Gaining

dedication

Christ has to be our ultimate goal. It takes humility to realize that apart from him we can do nothing.

Whatever Paul thought was personal gain prior to his conversion was afterward *counted* loss for Christ. Anything that hinders us from the excellency of the knowledge of Christ is worth losing. Paul was completely dedicated to Christ. To be dedicated to such a cause as Christ requires total consecration.

According to *Vine's Expository Dictionary of Biblical Words,* the verb "dedicate" means to make new, to renew, and to initiate. The first covenant was not dedicated without blood. The new covenant, through the blood of Jesus, is Christ's dedication of the new and living way. The noun "dedication" became used particularly for the annual eight days' feast known as the Feast of Dedication. It was instituted to commemorate the cleansing of the Temple from the pollutions of Antiochus Epiphanes. The lighting of the lamps was a prominent feature (Vine, 283). As we dedicate ourselves, we walk in newness of life. As we present our bodies as living sacrifices, we are cleansed from the works of the flesh.

This definition indicates the importance of consecration. We are to be the lights of the world, shining the glory of the Lord in every place. The more surrendered we are, the brighter we become. Dedication must manifest in our spirit, soul, and body. The cleansing of our body, our temple, is necessary in order to be an instrument in his hands. Our thoughts have to be taken captive to the obedience of Christ; like Paul, we must be willing to lose whatever we have gained that would hinder the Christ in us.

To dedicate something means to set it apart, to utilize it for a specific purpose, to give it over to a cause. When we dedicate our lives to the service of the Lord, we gradually learn to say no to whatever stops our yes to his call.

It is worth giving up whatever is needed for the call; nothing comes above what God has for us. Of course, it is through continual obedience that this is established, and there are many times we miss it in the process. During these times of failure, when our walk does not match our talk, we grow. If we respond to the Holy Spirit, his conviction will always lead us closer to the Lord. However, the condemnation of Satan will push us away and cause us to remain stuck in some areas while we grow in others. Focusing on the areas where we have progressed, we move forward. The problems increase in our sight and can quickly hinder the areas of victory when our eyes are on those areas that still need work. Our primary purpose is to be transformed into the image of Christ from glory to glory.

As we dedicate every area to him, we serve him wholly. Our level of dedication is seen through our walk. No matter what God is calling us to do, our primary purpose is to be transformed into the image of Christ from glory to glory; this transformation is demonstrated through our character. We cannot dedicate ourselves without dedicating our walk to him, from step to step, as follows.

1. Walk in Love

The love of God, *agape* in Greek, is unconditional and cannot be faked by Satan. It comes from our heart and is given by the Holy Spirit.

> And hope maketh not ashamed; because the love of God is shed abroad in our hearts by the Holy Ghost which is given unto us.
>
> Romans 5:5

Whatever gifts of the Holy Spirit flow through us, if we are without love, they are diminished to nothing.

> Jesus said unto him, Thou shalt love the Lord thy God with all thy heart, and with all thy soul, and with all thy mind. This is the first and great com-

mandment. And the second is like unto it, Thou shalt love thy neighbor as thyself.

> Matthew 22:37–39

Compassion flows out of love, and love conquers all, including fear that the enemy uses the most to hinder our walk. The more we grow in love, the less we retract. The degree to which we understand and receive his love for us, and what he did because of it, is the degree to which we will love him and therefore be able to love others and ourselves.

> We love him, because he first loved us.
> 1 John 4:19

When we love God and our neighbor but not ourselves, or love our neighbors and ourselves but not God, or we love God, ourselves, and not our neighbor, we open a door to the enemy. These three areas of love have to be covered: God, our neighbor, and ourselves. As we allow the Lord to heal our broken heart, we become whole.

> There is no fear in love; but perfect love casteth out fear: because fear hath torment. He that feareth is not made perfect in love.
> 1 John 4:18

Walking in love comes first before walking in truth and in the Spirit. It is the springboard to the manifestation of all the fruit of the Spirit and the evidence of our salvation. Love also helps us grow into him in all things.

> But speaking the truth in love, may grow up into him in all things, which is the head, even Christ.
>
> Ephesians 4:15

We should love one another in deed and in truth. When we truly walk in love, we will speak and walk in truth as he has.

2. *Walk in Truth*

This increasing transformation carries another evidence of character, which is integrity. Integrity will meet prosperity that will last for eternity. True prosperity in all areas of our lives will flourish as we do all in view of our eternal destiny. Many desire the prosperity of their finances but not of their souls, which in turn hinders their health. God's provision is for wholeness; as we seek first the kingdom, all necessary needs are met.

> Beloved, I wish above all things that thou mayest prosper and be in health, even as thy soul prosper-

eth. For I rejoiced greatly, when the brethren came and testified of the truth that is in thee, even as thou walkest in the truth. I have no greater joy than to hear that my children walk in truth.

3 John 2–4

It is truth in which we can prosper in all ways, and as prosperity is reached, that truth is manifested. The Greek for prosper is *eudeo,* which means to successfully reach. We are being restored to our original unbroken state that was evident before the fall of Adam and Eve. Being transformed by the renewing of our mind is prosperity of our soul. This wholeness is directly connected with truth in all areas of our lives. Integrity in what we do as ambassadors of Christ positions us to receive increase in all areas.

Webster's definition of *integrity* includes:

1. Wholeness; entireness; unbroken state. The Constitution of the Unites States guarantees to each state the integrity of its territories. The contracting parties guarantee the integrity of the empire.

2. The entire, unimpaired state of any thing, particularly of the mind; moral soundness or purity; incorruptness; uprightness; honesty. Integrity comprehends the whole moral character, but has a special

3. Purity; genuine, unadulterated, unimpaired state; as the integrity of language.

What I am expressing is the heart of God for such a time as this. Success in appearance only, not birthed from integrity of heart, will fall to nothing. As we heed the conviction of the Holy Spirit and yield to his reformation in any area where we have lied, stretched, omitted, hidden, twisted, or hindered truth in order to gain something, we will see a great exhibition of restoration. This applies to relationships, businesses, ministries, and any other field where growth has come but was not laid upon truth. Confession and repentance will clean past errors, and forgiveness will open a door to the "much more" of God. "Ishmael" prosperity, brought forth by the flesh, needs to be turned over to God in order for "Isaac" prosperity to be brought forth and released by the Spirit. To walk in our future, we have to walk in truth in all areas of our lives. Many secret sins are being revealed, and many will be healed. God desires to entrust much more into our lives. As we take heed to this word, many other words spoken over our lives will come to pass.

COUNTING THE COST

> Better is the poor that walketh in his integrity, than he that is perverse in his lips, and is a fool.
>
> Proverbs 19:1

It also reaches the next generations. The inheritance we leave is the integrity of his heart; our children are linked to it.

> The just man walketh in his integrity: his children are blessed after him.
>
> Proverbs 20:7

In looking at our heart, can God choose us as he did David?

> He chose David also his servant, and took him from the sheepfolds: From following the ewes great with young he brought him to feed his people, and Israel his inheritance. So he fed them according to and guided them by the skillfulness of his hands.
>
> Psalms 78:70–72

> Then said Jesus to those Jews who believed upon him, If ye continue in my word, then are ye my disciples indeed; And ye shall know the truth, and the truth shall make you free.
>
> John 8:31–32

Walking in truth will bring freedom from soul ties, lies, lack, oppression, depression, bondage, and many other things that have been hindering our walk as the new man.

3. *Walk in the Spirit*

Walking in the Spirit is evident when the inward work of the Holy Spirit is revealed outwardly. What is on the inside comes out under pressure. Stressful situations are allowed by God to bring to the surface what still needs to be healed. The opposite is true of the Spirit-led life: the fruit of the Spirit coming forth when tested demonstrates what has been perfected in hidden places. The fruit is exhibited by what has taken place on the inside.

> This I say then, Walk in the Spirit, and ye shall not fulfill the lust of the flesh.
>
> Galatians 5:16

> But the fruit of the Spirit is love, joy, peace, longsuffering, gentleness, goodness, faith, meekness, temperance: against such there is no law. And they that are Christ's have crucified the flesh with the affections and lusts. If we live in the Spirit, let us also walk in the Spirit. Let us not be desirous of vain glory, provoking one another, envying one another.
>
> Galatians 5:22–26

COUNTING THE COST

The work of the Spirit happens in the secret place. It cannot be faked or fabricated. We bear fruit; we cannot create it. As we abide in him and yield to his working *in* us, he can work *through* us. What is in private is being revealed in public.

The Spirit of Christ abiding in us results in an outflow of his characteristics. They increase as our flesh decreases. As the scripture indicates, the fruit is for those who are Christ's, who have crucified the flesh with its affections and lusts. Thus, to the degree in which we identify with his crucifixion, we can identify with his resurrection. The life of the Spirit emanates from the death of the flesh.

The new creature that we are in Christ manifests as the old man remains dead. When we walk in the Spirit, his character overflows. It eliminates vain glory, provoking one another, envying one another. In other words, three of the most devastating attitudes our carnal nature carries—comparing, criticizing, and complaining—give place to esteeming, exhorting, and being content in whatever state we are in. From faith to faith we seek less of our flesh so that more of his Spirit can flow through us. Could this be spiritual maturity?

> Brethren, I count not myself to have apprehended: but this one thing I do, forgetting those things which are behind, and reaching forth unto those things which are before, I press toward the mark for the prize of the high calling of God in Christ Jesus.
>
> Philippians 3:13–14

This scripture expresses what we should be reaching for. When what we try to achieve is the prize of the high calling of God in Christ Jesus, the decisions we make and the directions we take will be heaven bound. Our eyes are on the incorruptible crown, the crown of life, righteousness, and glory that fades not away. We are called to a kingdom in all glory. When we realize the greater glory laid ahead, all the steps in between will be from one level of glory to another. How did Paul reach beyond his reach? How can we?

First of all, as we read in Philippians 3:12, Paul did

destination

not think he had arrived. He said, "Not as though I had already attained, either were already perfect: but I follow after, if that I may apprehend that for which also I am apprehended of Christ Jesus."

Constantly knowing that there is more to attain is mandatory to growth. Understanding that we have not chosen Christ Jesus, but he has chosen us, breaks our pride and self-reliance. When I look at my past and see God's hand upon me when I didn't know him, I stand in awe of his care. It is he who apprehended me, not I who apprehended him. The full purpose for which I am his is yet to unfold. We are his workmanship, created in him for good works indeed. *Apprehended* comes from the Greek word *katalambano*. *Katalambano* comes from the word *kata*, meaning down, against, or according to, and the word *lambano*, meaning to take or receive. Together they mean to lay hold of as to make one's own, to obtain, to take into one's self, to appropriate, to seize upon, or take possession of.

Christ laid hold of us through the cross. All that he purchased for us on Calvary we have to appropriate in our lives. Our position in him now determines our provision. To possess what he has requires a continual pursuit, a following after those things that are above and not beneath. We have a glimmering view of it and are blessed with hope in it. No matter what we think God is doing, we quickly find out he is truly doing much more. It is as though we walk in a dot-to-dot game. With each step, a dot is connected and the picture gets clearer. However, it is often connected to yet another picture that is larger than we can see. Therefore, this first observation is the basis of our walk. Putting God in a box, assuming we know all things, and insisting on doing what *we* thought we were called to do will cause us to be stuck. Paul *counts* on God taking him from glory to glory. He knows he has not yet apprehended all for which God has apprehended him.

Secondly, Paul declares that there is one thing that he continually does. He forgets those things that are behind. Forgetting, in this context, means to loose from one's mind, to neglect, no longer care for a specific thing. What are we to forget? We know about the failures and mistakes we have to release. What is most difficult is to forget the successes. The ways we accomplished an assignment in the past might not necessarily work for what is laid ahead of us. The tendency is to trust what was successful rather than inquire of the Lord. However, the directives may or may not remain the same. This is true not only for what we have done ourselves, but also in relation to what others have completed. To copy what someone else has done and to think that we will obtain the same results is dangerous. We should not compare ourselves with another. The Spirit of Christ is a pioneer spirit. There is newness in doing what he calls us to do. He gives us our daily bread and does not want us to use yesterday's manna. We cannot follow him if our eyes are on yesterday. What happened then can hinder our future if we let it. Paul *counts* on that too; forgetting is necessary.

Thirdly, reaching forth is to be done in order to forget. We get this picture of Paul letting go of something that is behind him in order to grab hold of what is before him. Oftentimes when we do not know there is something ahead of us, we hang on to the past. Because what is in front of us is beyond our reach in the natural, it requires a stretching forth, a pulling forward, an assurance of the evidence of the things not seen. It is in the forgetting that we are able to do the reaching; they are intertwined.

What we reach for has to be more important to us than what we are required to let go of. That is where the battle rages. Because we are familiar and comfortable with what needs to be removed, we refuse to move into an unknown area and freeze in our steps; fear interferes. We wait for some proof that what is to come will turn out all right, but all we get is more doubt. Our trust cannot be in *what* we know but in *whom* we know. When we know him, our Master Jesus Christ, we would rather make every effort necessary to obey him than to never try at all. We are persistent in our endeavors. God will cause us to be moved to move. He will allow circumstances to push us forward. If we start with him, we can trust him to bring what he is doing to pass. If we start anything *counting* on ourselves, then when difficulties arise, we doubt his help because we know deep inside that we were asking him to follow us instead of us following him. But praise him forevermore that even in this case he pulls us out of our prideful decisions when we *count* on his mercy and grace in our time of need. The key is continued seeking of his will because it is easy to take things for granted. Let us remember not to step too soon into a situation when we have grown weary in waiting on God. Presumption is as much a sin as rebellion. *Rebellion* is not doing what we know God has told us to do. *Presumption* is to do in our own way what he told us to do.

Another obstacle in reaching is our assessing the size of what lies ahead as being too small. It is interesting that God tests our hearts by putting something little in front of us to see what we will do with it. The enemy's tactic is to intensify what he puts in our way when in fact it is small and powerless. God's way is to use the little that is in our hands and multiply it as we are faithful. He then gives us much more. I discovered that little is much in his hand. In obeying what he has asked me to do, I realized that nothing ever was what it appeared to be. For example, reaching out to one person was connected to many others. Helping another minister who did not have much was in fact a connection to an international ministry call. Going out of my way to obey simple instructions was actually putting me in the right direction for another matter. Oh, that we may never limit God with what we can see!

Another aspect of reaching is to move forward with "the little" yet always having the "much more" in view. Decisions cannot be made with subtraction in our calculations. Because God is a God of multiplication, we should not expect something not to grow. For example, in setting up phones for an office with four people, we should buy a system to which lines can be added, not a phone system that will only accommodate four employees. What we reach for will require withdrawals from deposits God has already made in our lives. The provision needed for what he has us reach for will come when we lay hold of it, not before. There are deposits made in our lives for things that are yet to come. Eye has not seen and ear has not heard of them yet. God sees the end from the beginning and waters our vineyard of today with the harvest of tomorrow in view.

Ac*count*ability is defined as the state of being liable

to answer for one's conduct; liability to give ac*count* and to receive reward or punishment for actions. We are ac*count*able to God, and will explain to him what we have done with what he has deposited into our lives at the judgment seat of Christ. Paul did what he did with eternity in view, and we should do the same. We should also surround ourselves with people to whom we can be ac*count*able. Because of this, in reaching for what God has apprehended me, I remind myself of two basic wisdom keys. The first is: *haste makes waste.* Anything I have to do in a hurry brings a check in my spirit. If I do not have time to consult with the Lord as his co-laborer, then it cannot be from him. Now this is different from the times when the Spirit of the Lord comes upon me to move suddenly. In those times, I realize afterward what he has done. The peace and surety that come cannot be faked by the enemy. The other key is: *when in doubt, don't.*

We cannot move in fear and faith at the same time. If I have any doubt about the direction I am to take, I stop, pray, and ask for divine wisdom as instructed in James 1:5. Divine wisdom is accompanied by peace and confidence. I wait and trust him to lead me as he wills.

Finally, Paul knew that using keys of the world would not open doors of the kingdom. Those doors are only accessible with kingdom principles. When God gives us a vision, he also releases the instructions along with the unction to function in every detail. There are several examples in the Bible where people were given specifics, like Noah for constructing the ark and Solomon for building the tabernacle. We can trust him to do the same for us.

Rest assured that God is able to speak loud enough for us to hear him, and as we acknowledge him in all our ways, he shall direct our paths. In observing Paul's life and many others' in the cloud of witnesses, we can be encouraged that if God used them, he can surely use us. The testimony of God is greater when we are not qualified, and he qualifies us. It has been said that God does not call the qualified but qualifies the called; by his grace we are called. By walking into what he has done for us in spite of us and having faith in him and not in ourselves, we are not only chosen but also called.

When something we reached for falls to nothing, we should rejoice. Not only the steps, but also the stops, are ordered by God. Over the years I had to remind myself often of what is written in Acts 5:38–39:

> And now I say unto you, Refrain from these men, and let them alone: for if this counsel or this work be of men, it will come to nought: But if it be of God, ye cannot overthrow it; lest haply ye be found even to fight against God.

So if the counsel or a work is of men and not of God, it will come to nothing. Therefore, when it does, I know that it was not of God. But when the work is of God, I trust that whatever battles are coming my way are against him and not me. The battle is then his, and I rest. What is of God cannot be overthrown! Hallelujah!

> My brethren, count it all joy when ye fall into divers temptations; knowing this, that the trying of your faith worketh patience. But let patience have her perfect work, that ye may be perfect and entire, wanting nothing.
>
> James 1:2–4

As we obey the call of God on our life, unforeseen difficulties arise. Our ability to win these battles is connected with foreseeing these trials as launching pads for our purpose. Foreseeing means we have ac*count*ed for it to happen. If we *count the cost* accurately, unexpected trials will be part of expected triumphs. The devil fighting us from the opposite direction is confirmation that we are going in the right direction.

The battles are not coming in opposition to where we are but to where we are going to be. Looking at our current state, we do not understand the intensity of the

divers temptations

war that comes against us. It is hard to imagine how what we have can cause such uproar. Our opponent is after the greater one who is in us. The more the anointing increases in and through us, the more hindrances are to be expected.

The battles are never because of natural happenings. If the enemy can cause us to focus on the problems related to relationships, jobs, money, material things, and other similar "earthly" things, we will not be able to release the anointing from within. Satan then throws fiery darts aimed at the outward to hinder the inward. He is most threatened when the Greater One who is within us is free to move. The battle then is truly the Lord's, and the explosion that comes forth destroys every mountain that is in the way and every yoke that slows us down. Victory is ours!

When we realize that the war is about stopping the glory that is within from coming out, the strength of the Lord is intensified. The Holy Spirit empowers us to face all trials with his ability, and we no longer react as we used to. Instead of fighting against flesh and blood we can perceive what is really happening in the spiritual realm and come against that specifically. Battling people around us is then replaced with attacking the enemy directly. When we perceive the real motive behind an action, we no longer waste time fighting what appears to be but finally address what truly needs to be overcome.

In other words, as the enemy tries to come against the anointing so that it will decrease, the opposite happens; it increases. We easily forget that.

> For we wrestle not against flesh and blood, but against principalities, against powers, against the rulers of the darkness of this world, against spiritual wickedness in high places.
>
> Ephesians 6:12

So the next time we face a battle, let's ask ourselves, "What is the *real* reason for this battle?" The divers temptations that James relates to are the various kinds of trials that we might experience. The key word is *various*. Attacks will come unexpectedly and from different sources. Diversity will come with adversity. The enemy will try to surprise us so that we do not see him coming. If we are used to war in one area only, we do not watch another. We need to always watch and pray. On a battlefield it is important to know when to fire, when not to fire, when to hide, and how to proceed. When the commander gives us instructions, we are to follow them, no questions asked. The tactics are similar in our spiritual warfare. Our king knows what to do to establish his kingdom. What he tells us to do rarely makes sense. What is the most valuable training tool he uses? Worship.

Intimacy in worship then becomes our most viable preparation point. It is in our worship that the war is won, the place in which we become filled with the right ammunition and receive instruction. Worship takes us into a higher realm whereby our fighting can be done from above, not beneath. All things are under our feet as we quench all the fiery darts of the enemy by stepping upon every lie. It is important to have a specific word for a specific situation. It is then that unspeakable joy, full of glory, floods our souls. When we war in the flesh we become agitated, yell, see the wrong anger expressed, say things we do not mean, and become worn out quickly with nothing accomplished. When we war in the Spirit, we know how to wait until we can battle by and with the Spirit. In quietness and in confidence comes strength.

We run to our time with the Lord so that only righteous anger comes forth, and what we speak are words of life, not death. Worship cannot be offered apart from prayer. So how do we pray?

In worship what we have received through the cross is revealed. In prayer we learn how to use what we have. Prayer, therefore, is one of our greatest weapons. Through it we obtain instructions on where to aim our sword, the Word of God. It is also through prayer that our helmet of salvation, breastplate of righteousness, belt of truth, shoes for the preparation of the gospel of peace, shield of faith, and sword of the Spirit are polished with his anointing. Oh, that prayer would not be seen as a way to ask God to give me all that I want but as a strategic meeting for battle! Our request should be, "What is it that you want, Lord? What can I do for you? What is your heart? What is your will?" We have a personal relationship with our God, and communication with him is how we grow into the knowledge of him. Worship and prayer are some of the major keys to the kingdom. The result of our worship and prayer will be obedience.

> For though we walk in the flesh, we do not war after the flesh: (For the weapons of our warfare are not carnal, but mighty through God to the pulling down of strongholds;) Casting down imaginations, and every high thing that exalteth itself against the knowledge of God, and bringing into captivity every thought to the obedience of Christ.
>
> 2 Corinthians 10:3–5

The imaginations that need to be destroyed are the ungodly thoughts we have not taken captive when they first came. It is like a chain reaction. One thought leads to another, then another, and so on, until it becomes a stronghold. It is intended to get us to the point of acting out the sin we are tempted by.

What we have reasoned, calculated, and concluded has more impact than what the Word of God says, and it must be destroyed. Although we have the mind of Christ, our carnal mind has been exercised for so long that it comes forth "naturally" and hinders the release of the supernatural. Therefore, we have to exercise the mind of Christ in order to war effectively. In this crucial battle, the first thought must be taken captive in order for the others to be conquered. When we agree with the first thought, it leads to disobedience, multiplies the deception, and causes us to do the very thing we do not want to do. As we replace it with a first thought of obedience like "I can do all things through Christ, which strengthens me," the opposite is true: my confession of faith will grow and obedience will follow.

Obedience to Christ must always be our target. We need to use our authority in Christ by taking captive every high thing that exalts itself against the knowledge of God. Whatever quenches our obedience to him must be exposed and overcome. Divine wisdom is connected with knowing God's thoughts and his ways, which are much higher than ours. What is from our nature needs to be brought low and destroyed so that the higher thoughts and ways that come from him are revealed.

Christ is our great captain in this warfare. In his name the battle is waged, and by his power the victory is won!

It is because we have the victory that we can *count* it all joy. We can be confident that the end result will be our wanting nothing, becoming perfect and entire. In other words, the divers temptations help us achieve what we are called to do completely, nothing missing.

If we know to expect these attacks and to rejoice in them, we will not be defeated when they come. When we say yes to the call, we have to *count on* the enemy fighting back. Then our *counting* is not on the devil's winning, but on our victory. We do not fight *for* victory but *from* the place of victory. On the cross, the battle was won; that is why the fight is a good fight of faith. It is God that is being fought, not us.

Can we *count* it all joy when we fall into those divers temptations? Yes, when we understand what our Lord Jesus Christ achieved for us. It is one thing to walk through a trial but another to endure it with joy. However, in doing so, the fruit of the Spirit will be seen as we continue to grow from glory to glory.

DR. JOELLE SUEL

> Rejoice, and be exceeding glad: for great is your reward in heaven: for so persecuted they the prophets which were before you.
>
> Matthew 5:12

We are to *count* it a matter of joy when our belief in the gospel is subjected to diverse trials. It is a good thing for us to have the reality of our faith tested any way necessary. The longer it takes to receive what we have believed God for, the greater the victory. If we do not let patience have her perfect work but intervene on our own behalf, something might happen that prevents us from receiving the perfect work God had for us. His extension is for our expansion. When I think of joy, I think of Paul, who took pleasure, meaning he jumped up and down with joy, in all that he endured. When Paul asked the Lord that his thorn in the flesh be removed, he heard and said this:

> And he said unto me, My grace is sufficient for thee: for my strength is made perfect in weakness. Most gladly therefore will I rather glory in my infirmities, that the power of Christ may rest upon me. Therefore I take pleasure in infirmities, in reproaches, in necessities, in persecutions, in distresses for Christ's sake: for when I am weak, then am I strong.
>
> 2 Corinthians 12:9–10

COUNTING THE COST

Let us never depend on our own strength, but when we have none, let us rejoice and *count* on his. The Greek word for strength is *dunamis,* which comes from the word *dunamai,* meaning to be able, or to have power. Its definition is miraculous power and might. In our weakness, our ability comes forth because of Christ in us. When we feel the weakest, we are the strongest because we are in him and he is in us. When we cannot, he can.

Christ in us is the hope of glory. The more we decrease, the more he increases! Praise him forevermore!

> But none of these things move me, neither count
> I my life dear unto myself, so that I might finish
> my course with joy, and the ministry, which I have
> received of the Lord Jesus, to testify the gospel of
> the grace of God.
>
> Acts 20:24

Paul's expression of not *counting* his life dear unto himself is used in comparison to Christ and his gospel and the time in which his life should be laid down for him. Paul was not moved by circumstances and made no ac*count* of them at all. His life was not dear to him but was dear to Christ. Are we prepared to serve God even if it means giving up our life? Not to *count* our life dear in the sense here indicated is the only way to be able to stand firm in our calling.

In 1 Kings 19, as the Prophet Elijah heard Jezebel say she wanted him to die, he heard the word, saw

||||| |
determination

himself dead, ran for his life, and wanted to die. The moment he placed his eyes on himself, the spirit of death, depression, and oppression came upon him. The word *dear* means costly, valuable. In *counting the cost* of the call, laying down our life for the sake of the gospel must be considered.

Furthermore, Paul said, "None of these things move me." What things? The bonds and afflictions that wait for him in every city. In our service to the Lord, we have to be steadfast and immovable. Fixity (the quality or state of being fixed; steadiness or permanence) of purpose, boldness, tenacity, courage, fearlessness, valor, firmness of purpose, vigor, stamina, and perseverance are necessary. Not giving up is how these character traits are sharpened. To give up is one of the temptations the enemy will bring our way most often. He lies to people about who they are to prevent them from doing what they are called to do. Paul is expressing that no matter what awaits him, he is prepared for anything. He cannot be moved from the hope of the gospel, the ministry of the Word, or his journey. His faith could not be shaken; fear could not enter him; nothing could abort his purpose. Nothing, not even the possibility of death, could move him away from following the leading of the Lord. Prior to this he said, "And now, behold, I go bound in the spirit unto Jerusalem, not knowing the things that shall befall me there: save that the Holy Ghost witnesseth in every city; saying that bonds and afflictions abide me" (Acts 20:22–23).

Paul was bound in the Spirit to go to Jerusalem. Being tied to what the Holy Spirit leads us to do will keep us anchored to his purpose. To the same degree that we are bound in the Spirit, we are able to say no to what is contrary to his purpose and tries to tie us down. We are bound in the Spirit when we are so compelled to do something that no one can stop us. With surety in our steps, we become fearless and move with holy boldness. Often, the way we recognize the call to do something is by trying to get away from it, but we cannot. The more we attempt to do something else, the more the leading to do that one thing grows. In other words, we cannot get away from the call; it keeps knocking at our door.

Paul knew by the Spirit of God that he should be laid in bonds, but the bonds he had with the Lord were stronger. He was steadfast and immovable. When we are bound to the covenant, bound to the spiritual realm, bound to his easy yoke, bound to him through the scarlet thread of his blood, no other bonds can tie us down. The unacceptable bonds will get disconnected one by one. We cannot be unequally yoked. That would hinder the call, quench the Holy Spirit, and move us away from finishing our course. Our relationships will be sifted one after the other. God knows the hidden weaknesses and protects us by cutting ties in our lives that cannot remain if we are to move forward.

To be determined is to be fully persuaded. Another biblical example is Abraham.

> By faith Abraham, when he was tried, offered up Isaac: and he that had received the promises offered up his only begotten son, of whom it was said, That in Isaac shall thy seed be called: Accounting that God was able to raise him up, even from the dead; from whence also he received him in a figure.
>
> Hebrews 11:18–19

Abraham was *count*ing on the fact that God was able to raise Isaac from the dead. That was the only outcome he could foresee. His conclusion was resurrection. *Counting* on that helped him go through what was facing him. He was so sure about it that he was ready to go through with offering up Isaac. We can say that we are ready to do whatever is asked of us, but to walk in it is another matter altogether. Even Peter said he would not deny the Lord, and yet he did. In order not to waver and to stay focused, we must guard what comes into us through the eyes, ears, and mouth. How so?

COUNTING THE COST

Regarding the eyes, what we behold will determine our outlook on things. What we dwell on, eventually we dwell in. Those things we see in the natural affect our thoughts and can cloud our decisions. Television programs or movies we watch must be carefully selected. Regarding the ears, what we hear is of great significance. We have to keep them closed to negative words and doubt and unbelief that come through others. Someone said that our ears are not garbage cans. When someone gossips or is very critical and uses our ears through their mouth to tear down instead of build up, we have to stop that person or remove ourselves from the situation as quickly as possible. Because of this, it is best not to tell everyone what the Lord is requesting of us. Last of all, our mouth needs to be guarded. God will show us what to share and what to keep quiet. The taming of our tongue will be tested in every step we take; controlling our words is a matter of life and death. We have to keep these openings naturally shut and spiritually attuned. Otherwise, our growth will be quenched.

Abraham looked ahead to the promise and did not look at the circumstances. He kept his mouth guarded and did not tell his wife. Abraham did tell his servants to stay at the bottom of the mountain, that he and the lad were going up to worship and would be coming back.

In doing so, he was confessing the outcome of the situation. Their coming through was not an issue to him. He kept his ears open to new instructions, so he was able to hear the angel tell him to stop. Abraham focused on what God could do instead of what he could do. We have to believe in the resurrection in order to walk in its power. Regardless of the commands or circumstances, we can determine to keep on keeping on.

It is through our determination that we will abound in the work of the Lord. Not much will be accomplished if we are not steadfast.

> The sting of death is sin; and the strength of sin is the law. But thanks be to God, which giveth us the victory through our Lord Jesus Christ. Therefore, my beloved brethren, be ye steadfast, unmovable, always abounding in the work of the Lord, forasmuch as ye know that your labor is not in vain in the Lord.
>
> 1 Corinthians 15:56–58

Unmovable, unbothered, unaffected, unshakable, bound to be determined, we are ambassadors of Christ.

And I will pray the Father, and he shall give you another Comforter, that he may abide with you for ever; Even the Spirit of truth; whom the world cannot receive, because it seeth him not, neither knoweth him: but ye know him; for he dwelleth *with* you, and shall be *in* you.

John 14:16–17

When he introduced the Holy Spirit, the third person of the Trinity, our Lord told us that he would dwell with us and be in us. He would be sent to execute all that was purchased for us on Calvary and would abide with us forever and reveal the truth to us. Before we were born again, the Holy Spirit was with us. Upon our conversion he dwells in us. His functions of conversion, illumination, and regeneration bring about transformation in our lives. The Holy Spirit convicts instead of condemns and comforts instead of crushes.

divine endowment

He draws us closer to his purpose instead of pushing us farther from it as he pulls us with gentleness and leads us- always from glory to glory. As his work is done on the inside, he proceeds to come upon us for work to be done on the outside. In addition to being *with* us and *in* us, he also comes *upon* us. This anointing upon us is for service. It is referred to in the following scriptures:

> But ye shall receive power, after that the Holy Ghost is come *upon* you: and ye shall be witnesses unto me both in Jerusalem, and in all Judea, and in Samaria, and unto the uttermost part of the earth.
>
> Acts 1:8

> And, behold, I send the promise of my Father *upon* you: but tarry ye in the city of Jerusalem, until ye be endued with power from on high.
>
> Luke 24:49

The promise of the baptism of the Holy Spirit is for every believer. Being endued with this power from on high is similar to sinking into a garment, to invest with clothing. To put on Christ is done as we put off the old man. *Christ* is the Greek word *Christos,* meaning anointed; that is, the Messiah. He is the anointed one, and through the Spirit of Christ in us, he operates through us as he wills. The Holy Spirit uses us; we do not use him. Indeed, we are the body of Christ. It is Christ in us that is the hope of glory.

The purpose of the anointing is to preach the gospel to the poor, to heal the brokenhearted, to preach deliverance to the captives, and recovering of sight to the blind, and to set at liberty them that are bruised.

I define the *anointing* as the manifestation of the power of the Holy Spirit in our lives. This divine endowment is the enablement Paul received as seen in 1 Timothy 1:12:

> And I thank Christ Jesus our Lord, who hath enabled me, for that he counted me faithful, putting me into the ministry.

The word *enabled* comes from the Greek word *endunamoo,* meaning to empower. One of the root words is *dunamis,* which describes a force or a miraculous power. In other words, it is not just being able to do something but being empowered to accomplish it as he would, not by might, nor power but by his spirit. This power is the manifestation of the Holy Spirit through us to do what we cannot do on our own. Truly God anoints those he appoints.

It is important that we define and connect being

faithful with being enabled. Paul was faithful because he believed in the reality of the Lord. This came as a result of his dramatic conversion on the road to Damascus. He was on his way to arrest those who had faith in the Lord when he was arrested by the Lord himself. His surrender was such that he asked the Lord: "What do you want me to do?" From that point on, he sought to do the will of God, regardless of the *cost*. Faithfulness is a necessary qualification for the ministry. We are made faithful and kept so by the grace of our Lord Jesus Christ. We are stewards of the manifold grace and mysteries of God. The more we realize this and all that comes from him, the more we cherish whatever he places in our hands. His faithfulness expands ours. We should be *so* grateful and humbled by his glory! As we are faithful with what he gives us, he multiplies it. We have to be good stewards of what God gives us, no matter how insignificant it appears to us.

Paul continued his tent making profession while he obeyed the Lord's direction and instruction. Knowing that the Lord can call upon us no matter where we are is crucial. Elisha was plowing, Moses was tending sheep, and the disciples had careers when they were apprehended for a specific purpose. Our Lord Jesus himself was occupied as a carpenter. We do not have to stop what we are doing to fulfill our purpose; we just need to be faithful where we are planted. The Lord will use whatever place or occupation we find ourselves in to fulfill his purpose. Many anointed believers are being used by God in the market place, releasing his glory!

To trust the Lord in spite of ourselves and to keep our eyes on whom he is in and through us rather than who we are in our flesh, are the main keys to our becoming trustworthy. When asked to watch over something that is not ours, we are oftentimes more careful than we would be with our own possessions. What an honor to walk circumspectly, with caution.

When our attitude is to go the extra mile in every endeavor, we advance in our spiritual journey. What a privilege to be his servant! Our reverent fear of God has to be greater than our fear of man. To know that what the Lord entrusts us with is his and not ours takes our ambassadorship to a new reality. We represent him and walk in increased ac*count*ability. When we receive a promotion in our place of work, we also accept more responsibility. It is so in the ministry.

The more that is given unto us, the more that is required. What is given to us is not revealed until after what is required has been completed. Therefore it is difficult to understand the *why* behind our circumstances. The more we give of what he has given us, the more we receive. With every increase comes a new level of authority. This is accompanied with a corresponding anointing.

We often only understand our lives by looking backward. How significant 1 Thessalonians 5:24 becomes: "Faithful is he that calleth you, who also will do it."

As God opens doors for us, all we can do is walk through them by faith. We are not to walk by sight. The empowerment will come when it is needed, not a second before. Again, the Holy Spirit uses us; we do not use him.

> But we have this treasure in earthen vessels, that the excellency of the power may be of God, and not of us.
>
> 2 Corinthians 4:7

Our part in co-laboring with him is to yield. We help him by not helping him. We surrender to his working, knowing that apart from him we really can do nothing; but because we are a part of him, with him all things are possible. The more we grow in Christ, the more 2 Corinthians 3:5 becomes reality: "Not that we are sufficient of ourselves to think any thing as of ourselves; but our sufficiency is of God."

Connecting being faithful and being enabled, I can truly proclaim, in accordance with the following:

COUNTING THE COST

Now unto him that is able to do exceeding abundantly above all that we ask or think, according to the power that worketh in us, Unto him be glory in the church by Christ Jesus throughout all ages, world without end. Amen.

Ephesians 3:20–21

conclusion

What a joy to be a bondservant of Christ! In *counting the cost*, it was all worth it. Above all, I gave my all for his all indeed. I continue to go from glory to glory, from faith to faith, from strength to strength. In his hands I rest. In his care I stand. In his Word I abide. In his love I remain. In his glory I glory. In him I live and move and have my being.

> For we are his workmanship, created in Christ Jesus unto good works, which God hath before ordained that we should walk in them.
> Ephesians 2:10

The good works that have been ordained for us are the result of his workings. As with a beautiful fabric, he connects each thread for the establishing of his kingdom. I give God praise, honor, and glory for joining us through these words and much more that we will one day see.

> Ye have not chosen me, but I have chosen you, and ordained you, that ye should go and bring forth fruit, and that your fruit should remain: that whatsoever ye shall ask of the Father in my name, he may give it you.
>
> John 15:16

As you read this book, I trust the Lord ministered to you. Never give in to the lies of the enemy in regard to who you are in Christ and who Christ is in you. To give in to those will lead you to give up. Keep on looking unto Jesus, the author and the finisher of your faith. As he has released confirmation, instruction, and revelation to you, remember that he will bestow upon you the anointing for the calling, the unction for every function. I exhort you to finish the race knowing your reward comes from him. As you make room for him, the gift makes room for you. Go forth in the name of Jesus! "Not by might, nor by power, but by the Spirit," says the Lord! Fight the good fight of faith! You are a winner, victorious in Christ! Mighty warrior, go forward no matter what the *cost* and whatever it takes!

My prayer for you is this:

> Wherefore also we pray always for you, that our God would count you worthy of this calling, and fulfill all the good pleasure of his goodness, and the

work of faith with power: That the name of our Lord Jesus Christ may be glorified in you, and ye in him, according to the grace of our God and the Lord Jesus Christ.

2 Thessalonians 1:11–12

nuggets of truth

Introduction

- What greater honor is there than to be a vessel of honor for the Lord of glory?

Chapter 1

- Death takes us into another realm of experiencing the reality of the life of Christ in us.

- The cross becomes the crossroad between the flesh and the Spirit.

- We *reckon* to have been crucified with Christ already but have to die daily to appropriate this great truth.

- When he becomes our motive for ministry, doors open for him, not us.
- We have to put off all of the body in order to put on all of Christ.

Chapter 2

- What we do portrays a greater message than what we say.
- We must become and remain teachable.
- Death to others does not mean that we are dead to others but that others are dead to us in the sense that they are no longer a source of life for us.
- Every relationship we have must be of a lesser priority than our relationship with him.
- The word that abides in me continues to grow as I let him add to it.

Chapter 3

- To be dedicated to such a cause as Christ requires total consecration.

COUNTING THE COST

- Our thoughts have to be taken captive to the obedience of Christ.

- Our primary purpose is to be transformed into the image of Christ from glory to glory.

- We are being restored to our original unbroken state that was evident before the fall of Adam and Eve.

- Success in appearance only, not birthed from integrity of heart, will fall to nothing.

- Thus, to the degree in which we identify with His crucifixion, we can identify with his resurrection.

Chapter 4

- Constantly knowing that there is more to attain is mandatory to growth.

- Our position in him now determines our provision.

- To copy what someone else has done and to think that we will obtain the same results is dangerous.

- Our trust cannot be in *what* we know but in *whom* we know.

- *Rebellion* is not doing what we know God has told us to do. *Presumption* is to do in our own way what he told us to do.

- Haste makes waste.

- When in doubt, don't.

- Divine wisdom is accompanied by peace and confidence.

- It has been said that God does not call the qualified but qualifies the called.

Chapter 5

- The battles are not coming in opposition to where we are but to where we are going to be.

- When we realize that the war is about stopping the glory that is within from coming out, the strength of the Lord is intensified.

- So the next time we face a battle, let's ask ourselves, "What is the *real* reason for this battle?"

- Attacks will come unexpectedly and from different sources. Diversity will come with adversity.

- It is in our worship that the war is won.

- In worship what we have received through the cross is revealed.

- Whatever quenches our obedience to him must be exposed and overcome.

- If we know to expect these attacks and to rejoice in them, we will not be defeated when they come.

- We do not fight *for* victory but *from* the place of victory.

- His extension is for our expansion.

Chapter 6

- Often, the way we recognize the call to do something is by trying to get away from it, but we cannot.

- The unacceptable bonds will get disconnected one by one.

- To be determined is to be fully persuaded.

- What we dwell on, eventually we dwell in.

- The taming of our tongue will be tested in every step we take; controlling our words is a matter of life and death.

Chapter 7

- Our reverent fear of God has to be greater than our fear of man.

- With every increase comes a new level of authority. This is accompanied with a corresponding anointing.

- As his work is done on the inside, he proceeds to come upon us for work to be done on the outside. This anointing upon us is for service.

- The Holy Spirit uses us; we do not use him.

- We help him by not helping him.

- The more we give of what he has given us, the more we receive.

- Unexpected trials will be part of expected triumphs.

COUNTING THE COST

Conclusion

- In his hands, I rest. In his care, I stand.
- In his Word, I abide. In his love, I remain.
- In his glory, I glory. In him, I live and move and have my being.

references

Strong, James. *Strong's Hebrew and Greek Dictionary.* (From Rick Meyers' e-sword.net)

Vine, W. E. *Vine's Expository Dictionary of Biblical Words.* (Nashville: Thomas Nelson, Inc., 1985), 283

Webster, Noah. *Noah Webster's Dictionary of American English,* 1828 Facsimile Edition. (Foundation for American Christian Education, 1967)

contact

For more information, you can contact Dr. Joelle Suel at:

http://drjoelle.tatepublishing.net

http://www.theglorioustruth.com